Juvenile

P9-EGL-051

Japanese Word Book

Yuko Green

with Preface by
Margaret Y. Yamashita

The Bess Press
P. O. Box 22388
Honolulu, HI 96823

Executive Editor: Ann Rayson
Design & Illustration: Yuko Green

Library of Congress

CATALOG CARD NO.: 89-91771

Green, Yuko
Japanese Word Book
Honolulu, Hawaii: Bess Press
112 pages   illustration, glossary-Japanese English, English Japanese

Hardcover ISBN: 1-880188-25-2
Paperback ISBN: 0-935848-74-6

TABLE OF CONTENTS

PREFACE

Japan has a rich heritage and culture which makes it unique. Although much is known about Japan, it remains a mystery in the eyes of many Westerners. Curiosity leads many to the study of the language. A recent survey by the Modern Language Association of America has shown that at the college level, the number of students studying Japanese has nearly doubled since 1986. However, all language educators know that starting the study of a foreign language at eighteen is too late. Ideally foreign language exposure occurs in childhood, the earlier the better. Bess Press of Hawaii has published The JAPANESE WORD BOOK in an attempt to respond to a lack of quality Japanese language materials at the elementary school level. The authentic while often entertaining illustrations by Yuko Green introduce the reader to the Japanese language in a fun and entertaining manner.

The author/illustrator, Yuko Green, is an artist and high school Japanese language teacher. Her combination of experience is clearly revealed by the authenticity of the illustrations as well as the sensitive choice of vocabulary items and manner of illustration. Revisions were made in this edition by the author in an effort to meet the needs of the readers and incorporate feedback received from educators in the field.

The words and phrases introduced encompass the basic aspects of Japanese society, because a language cannot be learned without the knowledge of the people and culture from which it springs. To know Japan, however, is not only to know its sleek modern buildings and high-speed trains. Modern Japan remains to this day with one foot in its cultural past: a world of traditional arts, esthetics, and values. To this end, the JAPANESE WORD BOOK juxtaposes old and new, traditional and modern images of Japan and captures the blend that forms the fabric of Japanese culture. Japanese traditional life-style is colorfully depicted in detailed drawings of traditional clothing, architecture, home furnishings, foods, sports and the arts. At the same time, contemporary Japan is seen in realistic drawings of means of transportation, clothing, and locations and activities in the urban setting. Basic greetings and expressions are also entertainingly presented. As a result, one finds in the JAPANESE WORD BOOK a perfect first-time language experience that is highly recommended for the young and young at heart.

Margaret Y. Yamashita
Japanese Language Program Coordinator
Japan-America Institute of Management Sciences

INTRODUCTION

The JAPANESE WORD BOOK is a fully illustrated introduction to both the language and culture of Japan for everyone, child and adult, student and teacher alike.

1. 310 common and basic Japanese words and phrases have been selected. While an effort was made to include words which show the unique characteristics of Japanese life and culture, the vocabulary will be a useful supplement to the word lists normally found in beginning Japanese language books.
2. The words and phrases are shown in visual form so that the reader will be able to translate the Japanese words and characters simply by looking at the pictures.
3. To make these unique Japanese terms clear and understandable, one picture is worth a thousand words of explanation. Teachers can use the JAPANESE WORD BOOK as a visual aid to supplement their existing course material and to enhance visually the students' learning.

What makes Japan so unique? It has a contemporary look on one side and yet still keeps a strong traditional look on the other. To learn a language one has to understand the cultural background. My primary goal was to show Japan in an old and new, traditional and modern setting, to reflect the language's strong connection with culture.

Above all, I hope that through the entire book the reader will experience this rich heritage of Japan and also meet its language effectively and enjoyably.

Acknowledgement

I wish to acknowledge the following people for their assistance and encouragement: first, I want to acknowledge Benjamin E. Bess of the Bess Press for making this edition possible; Dr. Margaret Y. Yamashita, Japanese Language Program Coordinator at Japan–America Institute of Management Sciences, for writing the Preface for this edition and for helping with the proofreading of the final materials; Mebane A. Boyd and Mauree D. Donahue of Hawaii Preparatory Academy, who have given so many suggestions from their experience of teaching.

Also, I wish to thank the many teachers who provided me with valuable feedback and advice on improving the first edition. All their help has made this edition better.

Yuko S. Green

PRONUNCIATION

Japanese words are made up of syllables based on 5 fundamental vowel sounds:

       a as in f<u>a</u>ther
       i as in mach<u>i</u>ne
       u as in fl<u>u</u>
       e as in <u>e</u>nd
       o as in <u>o</u>pen

Each syllable consists of a vowel, or of a vowel and a consonant, with the exception of **n** and/or **m**; these consonant sounds stand alone without a vowel sound (e.g.: te<u>n</u>pura/te<u>m</u>pura).
Each syllable is given equal value (stress and time) in pronunciation (i.e.: o–su–shi, o–ri–ga–mi).

Long vowel sounds are simply written as: **aa, ii, uu, ee, oo** in this revised version for beginners; this changes the length of the vowel.

The double consonant in Romanized Japanese words appears as small つ in Hiragana. This つ is one syllable in length, and there is the slightest pause between these two consonants (e.g.: gakkoo).

EXPLANATORY NOTES

Verbs. In this book the –**masu** form of the verb is given only in the vocabulary lists of IV.Verbs (p.17); elsewhere, the "plain present" form, often called "dictionary" form, is given.

Adjectives. The adjectives are in their "plain present" form.

Nouns. Japanese does not make a distinction between the singular and the plural. For instance, *kodomo* means both child and children. In this book English translations for nouns are put in the singular.

Prefix: (o) indicates an optional politeness marker which is not a part of the word itself (e.g. (o)sushi). However, it is written as a part of the word in cases where (o) is no longer optional (e.g. ocha) In the glossaries, words are alphabetized without (o).
Suffix: (san) indicates a politeness marker not necessarily a part of the word itself.

Arrangement

The book groups 310 words into 13 sections, such as family and relations, locations, verbs, adjectives, school, city, food, clothing, transportation and sport. Each section contains a vocabulary list.

At the beginning of the book is a writing and pronunciation guide that explains and presents three kinds of Japanese writing: 1. **Hiragana**, 2. **Kanji**, and 3. **Katakana**. Next to each illustration in the text are the romanized pronunciation and spelling of the Japanese word: two ways of writing these words in Japanese, the Hiragana and Kanji, or Katakana; and the English word. At the end of the book are the Japanese and English glossaries with translations.

There are three kinds of Japanese writing:

1. **Hiragana:** A phonetic syllabary.
2. **Katakana:** A second phonetic syllabary used for foreign words brought into Japan.
3. **Kanji:** Chinese characters, each expressing a meaning.

Written Japanese uses all three as appropriate.
The following is a chart of the Japanese syllables with their hiragana and katakana system of writing.

The *kana* to the left are *hiragana; katakana* are in parentheses.

I Basic Syllables: Vowel, consonant plus vowel and n

C \ V	a あ (ア)	i い (イ)	u う (ウ)	e え (エ)	o お (オ)
k	k a か (カ)	k i き (キ)	k u く (ク)	k e け (ケ)	k o こ (コ)
s	s a さ (サ)	s h i し (シ)	s u す (ス)	s e せ (セ)	s o そ (ソ)
t	t a た (タ)	c h i ち (チ)	t s u つ (ツ)	t e て (テ)	t o と (ト)
n	n a な (ナ)	n i に (ニ)	n u ぬ (ヌ)	n e ね (ネ)	n o の (ノ)
h	h a は (ハ)	h i ひ (ヒ)	f u ふ (フ)	h e へ (ヘ)	h o ほ (ホ)
m	m a ま (マ)	m i み (ミ)	m u む (ム)	m e め (メ)	m o も (モ)
y	y a や (ヤ)		y u ゆ (ユ)		y o よ (ヨ)
r	r a ら (ラ)	r i り (リ)	r u る (ル)	r e れ (レ)	r o ろ (ロ)
w	w a わ (ワ)				o を (ヲ)
n	ー ん (ン)				

II. Modified Syllables: Consonant plus basic vowel

g	g a が (ガ)	g i ぎ (ギ)	g u ぐ (グ)	g e げ (ゲ)	g o ご (ゴ)
z	z a ざ (ザ)	j i じ (ジ)	z u ず (ズ)	z e ぜ (ゼ)	z o ぞ (ゾ)
d	d a だ (ダ)			d e で (デ)	d o ど (ド)
b	b a ば (バ)	b i び (ビ)	b u ぶ (ブ)	b e べ (ベ)	b o ぼ (ボ)
p	p a ぱ (パ)	p i ぴ (ピ)	p u ぷ (プ)	p e ぺ (ペ)	p o ぽ (ポ)

III. Modified Syllables: Consonant plus ya, yu, yo

k y a きゃ (キャ)	k y u きゅ (キュ)	k y o きょ (キョ)
s h a しゃ (シャ)	s h u しゅ (シュ)	s h o しょ (ショ)
c h a ちゃ (チャ)	c h u ちゅ (チュ)	c h o ちょ (チョ)
n y a にゃ (ニャ)	n y u にゅ (ニュ)	n y o にょ (ニョ)
h y a ひゃ (ヒャ)	h y u ひゅ (ヒュ)	h y o ひょ (ヒョ)
m y a みゃ (ミャ)	m y u みゅ (ミュ)	m y o みょ (ミョ)
r y a りゃ (リャ)	r y u りゅ (リュ)	r y o りょ (リョ)
g y a ぎゃ (ギャ)	g y u ぎゅ (ギュ)	g y o ぎょ (ギョ)
j a じゃ (ジャ)	j u じゅ (ジュ)	j o じょ (ジョ)
b y a びゃ (ビャ)	b y u びゅ (ビュ)	b y o びょ (ビョ)
p y a ぴゃ (ピャ)	p y u ぴゅ (ピュ)	p y o ぴょ (ピョ)

I. Social Life and Relations

1. Family Relations

My	Your; Other's
chichi	otoosan *
haha	okaasan *
ani	oniisan *
ane	oneesan *
otooto	otootosan
imooto	imootosan
sofu	ojiisan *
sobo	obaasan *
oji	ojisan *
oba	obasan *
musuko	musukosan
musume	musumesan

Note: In Japanese there is a clear distinction between my family and your (or someone else's family) as shown above. However, * these words are also used within the family (see p.5).

2. Social Relations

akachan

anata

boku

gaijin, gaikokujin ✗

kodomo

nihonjin

onna

onna no hito

onna no ko

otona

otoko

otoko no hito

otoko no ko

(o) toshiyori, roojin

watashi

watashitachi

KAZOKU: かぞく，家族

family

KAZOKU (Within Family)

OJIISAN:
おじいさん
grandfather

OBAASAN:
おばあさん, お婆さん
grandmother

OJIISAN:
おじいさん
grandfather

OBAASAN:
おばあさん, お婆さん
grandmother

OJISAN:
おじさん
uncle

OKAASAN:
おかあさん, お母さん
mother

OTOOSAN:
おとうさん, お父さん
father

OBASAN:
おばさん
aunt

*

*

ONIISAN:
おにいさん,
お兄さん
older brother

ONEESAN:
おねえさん,
お姉さん
older sister

* Note:
Younger siblings are called by their names.

5

KAZOKU

2. Social Relations

OTOKO: おとこ, 男
male

OTOKO NO HITO:
おとこのひと, 男の人
man

OTOKO NO KO:
おとこのこ, 男の子
boy

ONNA: おんな, 女
female

ONNA NO HITO:
おんなのひと, 女の人
woman

ONNA NO KO:
おんなのこ, 女の子
girl

OTONA: おとな, 大人
adult

(O) TOSHIYORI:
おとしより, お年寄り
old person

KODOMO: こども, 子供
child

AKACHAN:
あかちゃん, 赤ちゃん
baby

OTOKO NO KO:
おとこのこ, 男の子
boy

ONNA NO KO:
おんなのこ, 女の子
girl

NIHONJIN:
にほんじん，日本人
Japanese

GAIJIN:
がいじん，外人
foreigner

II. Relative Locations

chikaku
hidari
mae
migi
naka
shita
soto
tooku
ue
ushiro

MAE: まえ, 前
front

USHIRO: うしろ, 後ろ
back

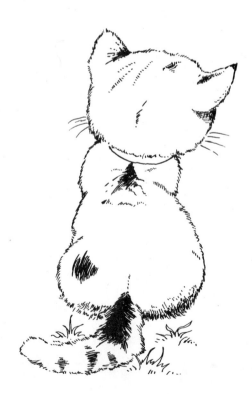

UE: うえ, 上
over

SHITA: した, 下
under

NAKA: なか, 中

inside

SOTO: そと, 外

outside

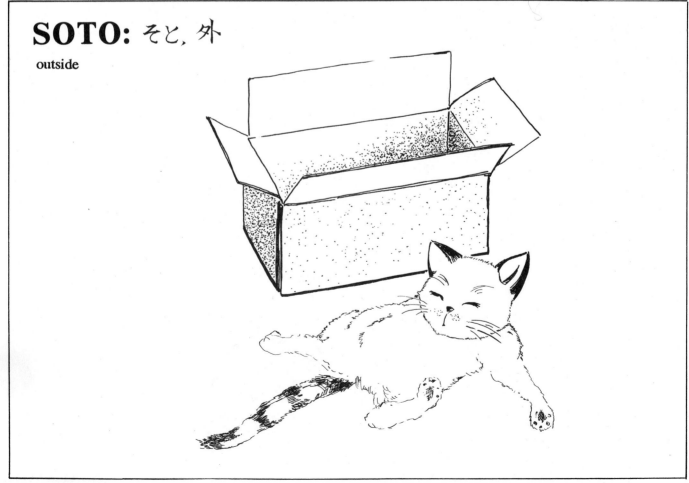

MIGI: みぎ, 右
right

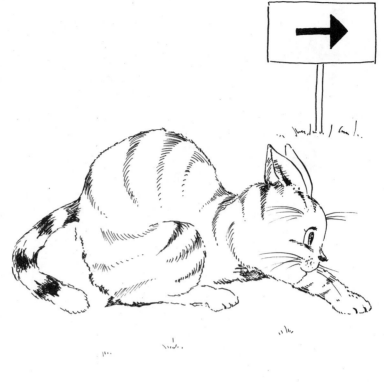

HIDARI: ひだり, 左
left

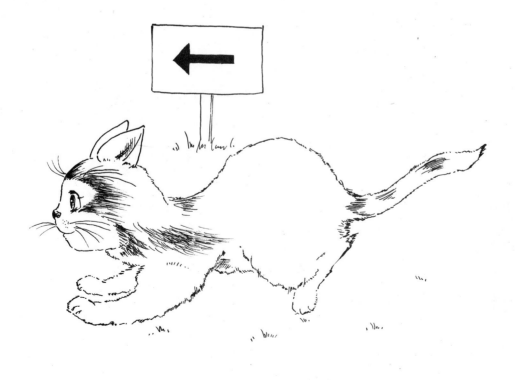

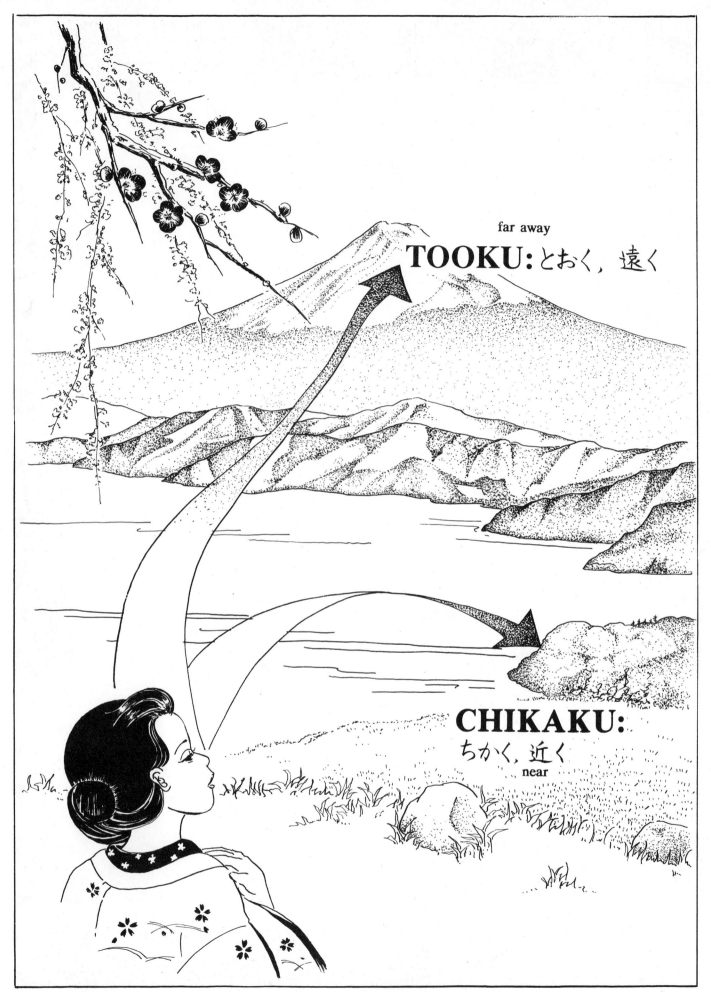

TOOKU: とおく，遠く
far away

CHIKAKU:
ちかく，近く
near

II. Verbs

agemasu (ageru)
akemasu (akeru)
arukimasu (aruku)
benkyoo (o) shimasu (benkyoo (o) suru)
denwa (o) shimasu (denwa (o) suru)
hakimasu (haku)
hanashimasu (hanasu)
hatarakimasu (hataraku)
shigoto (o) shimasu (shigoto (o) suru)
ikimasu (iku)
kaerimasu (kaeru)
kaimasu (kau)
kakimasu (kaku)
kangaemasu (kangaeru)
kikimasu (kiku)
kimasu (kuru)

mimasu (miru)
moraimasu (morau)
nemasu (neru)
nomimasu (nomu)
norimasu (noru)
nugimasu (nugu)
okimasu (okiru)
orimasu (oriru)
oshiemasu (oshieru)
shimemasu (shimeru)
suwarimasu (suwaru)
tabemasu (taberu)
tachimasu (tatsu)
urimasu (uru)
yomimasu (yomu)

Note: The verbs outside the parentheses show the —**masu** form;
inside is the —**u** form, which is less formal than the
—**masu** form.

TATSU: たつ, 立つ

to stand up

SUWARU: すわる, 座る

to sit down

ARUKU: あるく, 歩く

to walk

HASHIRU: はしる, 走る

to run

KAKU: かく, 書く
to write

YOMU: よむ, 読む
to read

SHINBUN:
しんぶん, 新聞
newspaper

TABERU: たべる, 食べる

to eat

NOMU: のむ, 飲む

to drink

HANASU: はなす, 話す
to speak

DENWA (O) SURU: でんわ（を）する, 電話（を）する
to phone

"MOSHI MOSHI!": もしもし Hello.

DENWA: でんわ, 電話
telephone

MIRU: みる, 見る

to watch

KIKU: きく, 聞く

to listen

OSHIERU: おしえる, 教える
to teach

BENKOYOO (O) SURU:
べんきょう（を）する, 勉強（を）する
to study

KANGAERU:
かんがえる, 考える
to think

HATARAKU:
はたらく, 働く
to work

AGERU: あげる
to give

MORAU: もらう 貰う
to receive

URU:
うる, 売る
to sell

KAU:
かう, 買う
to buy

AKERU: あける, 開ける
to open

SHIMERU: しめる, 閉める
to shut

あける, 開ける

IKU: いく, 行く
to go

KAERU:
かえる, 帰る
to return

KURU:
くる, 来る
to come

ORIRU:
おりる, 降りる
to get off

NORU:
のる, 乗る
to get on

KIRU: きる, 着る

to wear

HAKU: はく, 履く

to put on

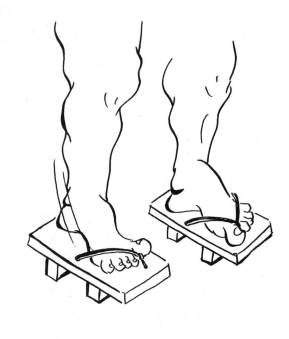

NUGU: ぬぐ, 脱ぐ

to take off

きる

NERU:
ねる, 寝る
to sleep

OKIRU:
おきる, 起きる
to get up

WARAU: わらう、笑う
to laugh

UTAU: うたう、歌う
to sing

IV. Adjectives

atarashii	mijikai	shizuka (na)*
atsui	muzukashii	takai
chiisai	nagai	tsumaranai
furui	oishii	tsumetai
hayai	omoi	urusai
hikui	omoshiroi	usui
ii	ookii	warui
karui	osoi	yasashii
kitanai	samui	yasui
kirei (na)*		

Note: All are adjectives except for those marked (*),
which are adjectival nouns.

TSUYOI: つよい, 強い

strong

YOWAI:
よわい, 弱い

weak

OOKII:
おおきい, 大きい
big

CHIISAI:
ちいさい, 小さい
small

KARUI:
かるい, 軽い
light

OMOI:
おもい, 重い
heavy

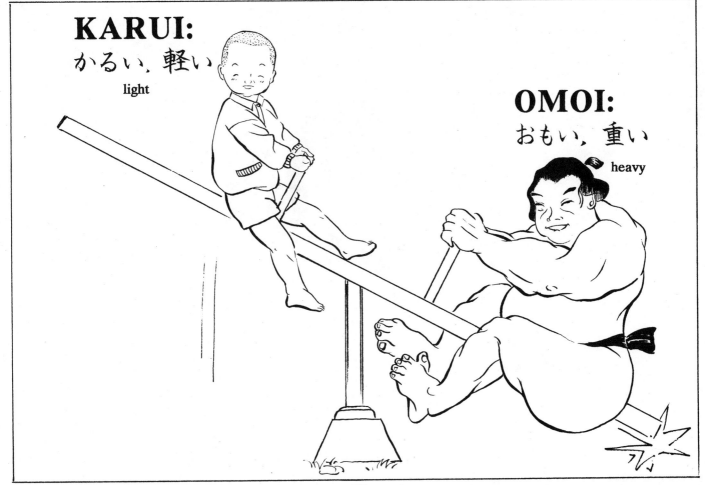

YASASHII: やさしい，易しい
easy

MUZUKASHII: むずかしい，難しい
difficult

MIJIKAI:
みじかい, 短い
short

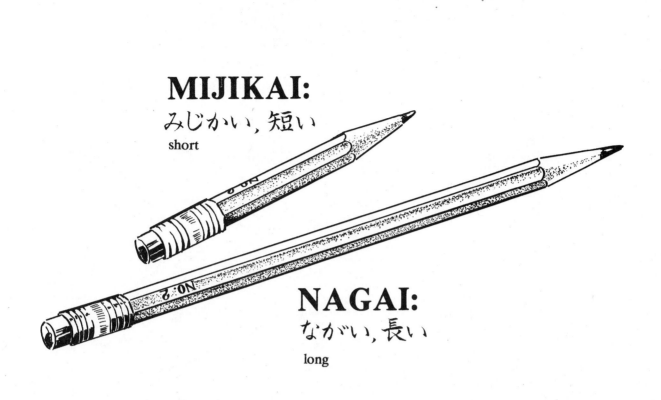

NAGAI:
ながい, 長い
long

II: いい, (良い)
good

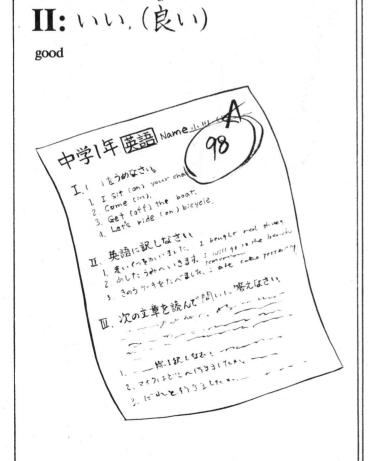

WARUI: わるい, 悪い
bad

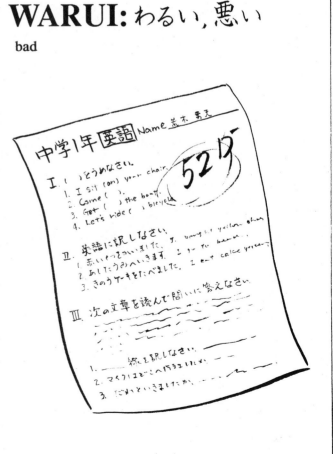

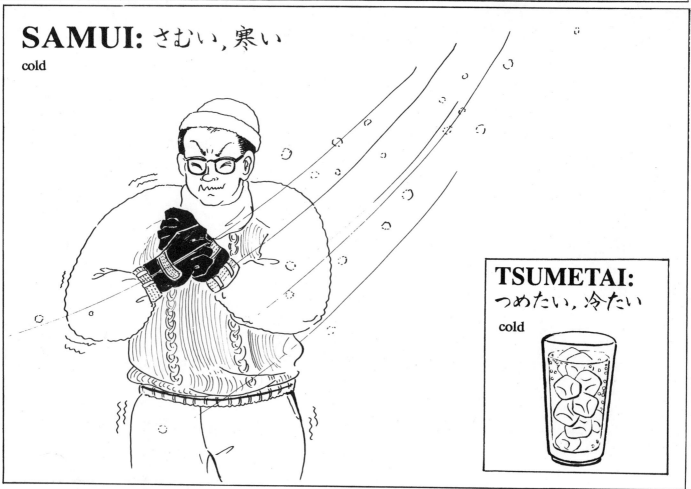

ATSUI: あつい, 厚い

thick

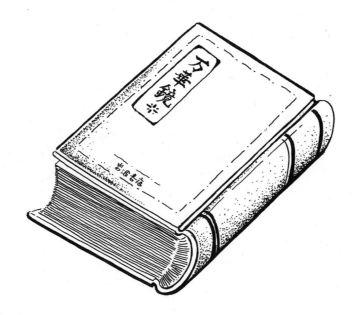

USUI: うすい, 薄い

thin

TAKAI: たかい, 高い
high

HIKUI:
ひくい, 低い
low

TAKAI: たかい，高い
expensive

YASUI: やすい，安い
cheap

KIREI (NA): きれい (な), 綺麗 (な)
beautiful, clean

KITANAI: きたない，汚ない
dirty

ATARASHII: あたらしい, 新しい

new

FURUI: ふるい, 古い

old

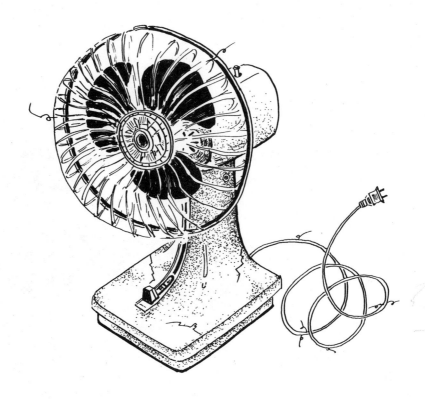

HAYAI: はやい, 早い

fast

OSOI: おそい, 遅い

slow

URUSAI: うるさい
noisy

SHIZUKA (NA):
しずか(な), 静か(な)
quiet

OMOSHIROI: おもしろい、面白い

interesting

TSUMARANAI: つまらない

boring

V. Japanese Lifestyle & Culture

1. House
futon
genkan
daidokoro
denki
e
hana
ha
ie
ike
ishi
ki
mado
makura
ningyoo
niwa
ofuro
otearai
terebi
to
tokei
yane

2. Town/City
byooin
dooro
eki
ginkoo
keisatsu
kippu
kitte
kooen
koosaten
kusuri
machi
okane
shingoo
suupaa
tegami
yakkyoku
yuubinkyoku

3. School
enpitsu
gakkoo
hon
isu
jisho
kami
kokuban
pen
seito, gakusei
sensei
shiken
toshokan
tsukue
yoochienji
shoogakusei
chuugakusei
kookoosei
daigakusei

4. Food
(o)bentoo
chawan
gohan
hashi
(o)kashi
koppu
kudamono
miso shiru
mizu
niku
nomimono
ocha
owan
sakana
(o)sake
sara
(o)sashimi
sukiyaki
(o)sushi
tabemono
tamago
tenpura
tsukemono
yunomi
yakitori
yasai

5. Clothing
booshi
burausu
fuku
geta
hankachi
kaban
kimono
kushi
kutsu
kutsushita
megane
obi
shatsu
sukaato
yukata
yoofuku
zoori
zubon

6. Traditions
bonsai
origami
ninja
samurai
shoogun
shuuji, shodoo

1. IE いえ, 家
house

YANE: やね, 屋根
roof

MADO: まど, 窓
window

TO: と, 戸 ア
door

GENKAN:
げんかん, 玄関
entrance hall

DAIDOKORO:
だいどころ, 台所
kitchen

OFURO:
おふろ, お風呂
bath

OTEARAI:
おてあらい, 御手洗い
bathroom

DENKI: でんき, 電気
electric light

E: え, 絵
picture

NINGYOO:
にんぎょう, 人形
doll

TOKEI:
とけい, 時計
clock, watch

MAKURA: まくら, 枕
pillow

FUTON: ふとん, 布団
comforter

NIWA:
にわ, 庭

garden

HANA: はな, 花

flower

IKE: いけ, 池

pond

ISHI: いし, 石

rock

KI: き, 木

tree

HAPPA: はっぱ, 葉っぱ

leaf

2. *MACHI*: まち, 街

town

traffic light

SHINGOO:
しんごう, 信号

DOORO:
どうろ, 道路
road

intersection
KOOSATEN:
こうさてん, 交差点

KEISATSU: けいさつ, 警察
police station

BYOOIN: びょういん, 病院
hospital

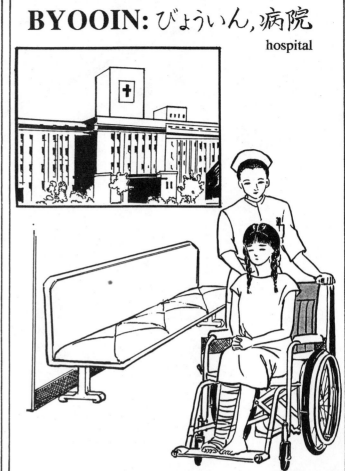

SUUPAA: スーパー
supermarket

KOOEN: こうえん, 公園　park

GINKOO:
ぎんごう, 銀行
bank

知多信用金庫

OKANE: (お)かね, (お)金
money

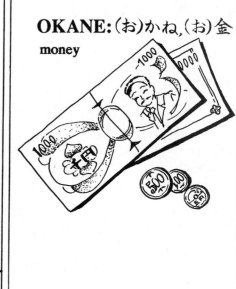

YUUBINKYOKU: ゆうびんきょく, 郵便局
post office

半田郵便局

郵便
POST

TEGAMI: てがみ, 手紙
letter

KITTE: きって, 切手
stamp

EKI: えき, 駅

train station

KIPPU: きっぷ, 切符

ticket

YAKKYOKU:

やっきょく, 薬局

pharmacy

KUSURI: くすり, 薬

medicine

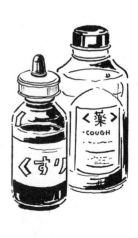

3. GAKKOO: がっこう, 学校
school

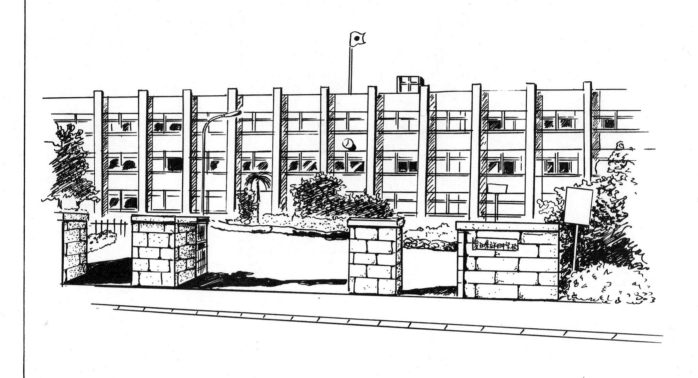

SENSEI:
せんせい, 先生
teacher

SEITO: せいと, 生徒
student

KOOKOOSEI:
こうこうせい, 高校生
senior high school student

DAIGAKUSEI:
だいがくせい, 大学生
college student

CHUUGAKUSEI: ちゅうがくせい, 中学生
junior high school student

SHOOGAKUSEI: しょうがくせい, 小学生
elementary school student

YOOCHIENJI: ようちえんじ, 幼稚園児
kindergartener

TSUKUE: つくえ, 机
desk

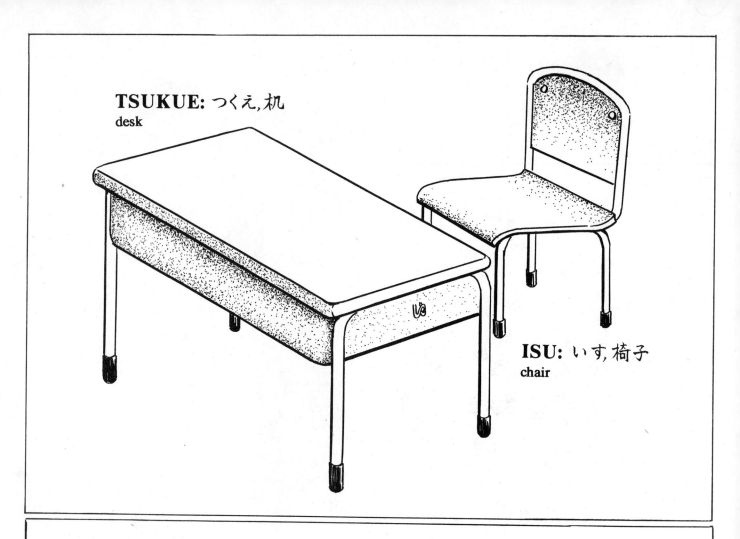

ISU: いす, 椅子
chair

KOKUBAN: こくばん, 黒板
blackboard

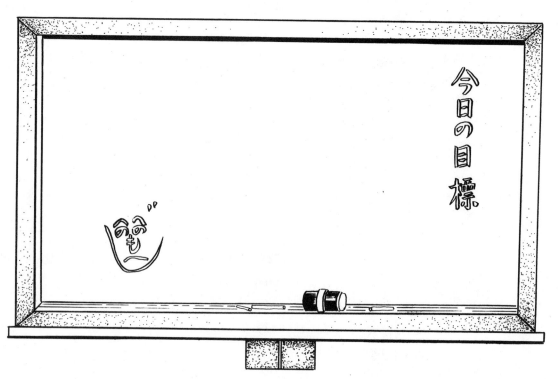

今日の目標

ENPITSU: えんぴつ, 鉛筆
pencil

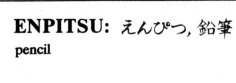

PEN: ペン
pen

HON: ほん, 本
book

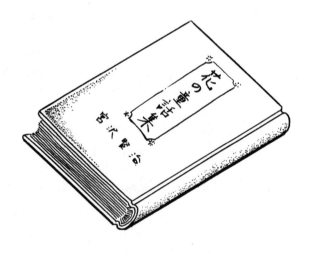

JISHO: じしょ, 辞書
dictionary

SHIKEN: しけん, 試験
test

KAMI: かみ, 紙
paper

4. TABEMONO: たべもの, 食べ物

food

(O) SAKE: （お）さけ, （お）酒
Japanese rice wine

SUKIYAKI:
すきやき, 好焼き
beef cooked with vegetables

TENPURA:
てんぷら, 天ぷら
deep-fried fish
and vegetables

(O) SASHIMI:
（お）さしみ,
（お）刺身
raw fish

(O) SUSHI: （お）すし, （お）寿司
vinegared rice with raw fish

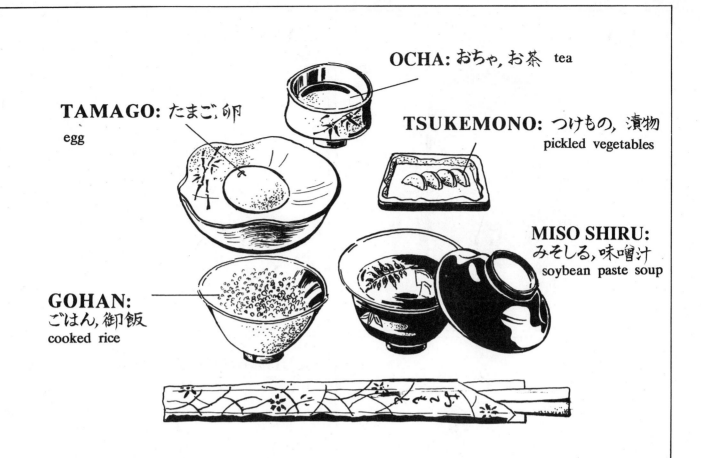

OCHA: おちゃ, お茶 tea

TAMAGO: たまご, 卵
egg

TSUKEMONO: つけもの, 漬物
pickled vegetables

MISO SHIRU:
みそしる, 味噌汁
soybean paste soup

GOHAN:
ごはん, 御飯
cooked rice

(O) BENTOO: (お)べんとう, (お)弁当
box lunch

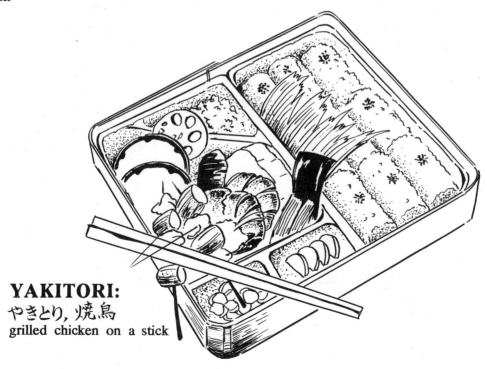

YAKITORI:
やきとり, 焼鳥
grilled chicken on a stick

NIKU: にく, 肉

meat

SAKANA: さかな, 魚

fish

YASAI: やさい, 野菜

vegetable

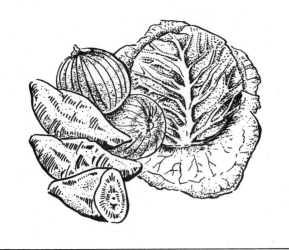

KUDAMONO: くだもの, 果物

fruit

(O) KASHI: (お)かし, (お)菓子

snack

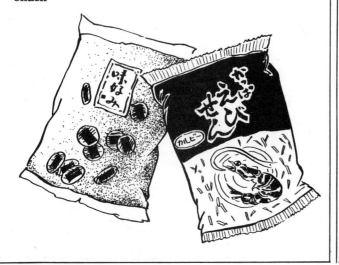

NOMIMONO: のみもの, 飲み物

drink

62

CHAWAN: ちゃわん, 茶椀
rice bowl

OWAN: おわん
soup cup

SARA: さら, 皿
dish

YUNOMI: ゆのみ, 湯呑み
tea cup

HASHI: はし, 箸
chopstick(s)

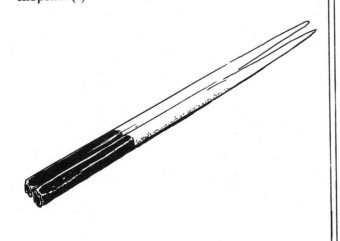

KOPPU: コップ
glass

5. *FUKU*: ふく, 服
clothes

KIMONO: きもの, 着物
Japanese clothing

OBI: おび, 帯
sash

YUKATA:
ゆかた, 浴衣
summer
cotton kimono

ZOORI: ぞうり
sandals

GETA: げた
wooden clogs

YOOFUKU: ようふく, 洋服
clothes

SHATSU: シャツ
shirt

BURAUSU:
ブラウス
blouse

SUKAATO:
スカート
skirt

ZUBON: ズボン
trousers

KUTSU: くつ, 靴
shoe(s)

KABAN: かばん, 鞄
bag

BOOSHI: ぼうし, 帽子
hat

KUTSUSHITA: くつした, 靴下
socks

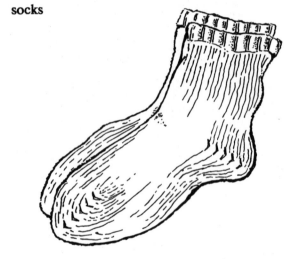

HANKACHI: ハンカチ
handkerchief

MEGANE: めがね, 目鏡
eyeglasses

KUSHI: くし, 櫛
comb

6. DENTOO: でんとう, 伝統

tradition

Japanese assassin
NINJA:
にんじゃ 忍者

general
SHOOGUN:
しょうぐん, 将軍

Japanese swordsman
SAMURAI:
さむらい, 侍

SHODOO: しょどう, 書道
SHUUJI: しゅうじ, 習字 calligraphy

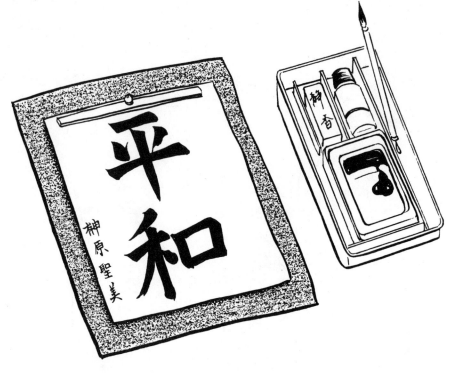

ORIGAMI: おりがみ, 折紙
paper-folding

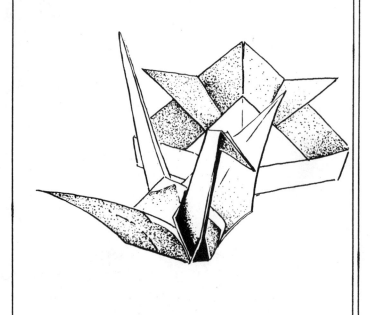

BONSAI: ぼんさい, 盆栽
miniature potted plant

VI. Transportation

basu
basutei
chikatetsu
densha
fune
hikooki
jitensha
kisha
kuruma, jidoosha
kuukoo
norimono
ootobai
shinkansen

KURUMA: くるま, 車

car

BASU: バス

bus

BASUTEI:
バスてい,
バス停

bus stop

JITENSHA: じてんしゃ, 自転車
bicycle

OOTOBAI: オートバイ
motorcycle

SHINKANSEN: しんかんせん, 新幹線

bullet train

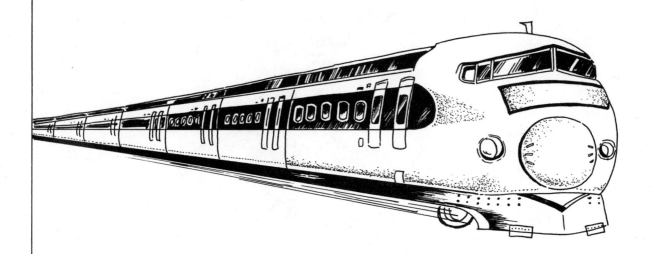

DENSHA: でんしゃ, 電車

electric train

CHIKATETSU: ちかてつ、地下鉄
subway

KISHA: きしゃ、汽車
freight train

HIKOOKI: ひこうき, 飛行機
plane

KUUKOO: くうこう, 空港
airport

FUNE: ふね, 船/舟
ship

VII. Sports

basuketto
gorufu
juudoo
kendoo
saafin
sukii
sumoo
tenisu
yakyuu

SUMOO:すもう, 相撲

Japanese wrestling

KENDOO:けんどう, 剣道

Japanese art of self-defense

76

JUUDOO: じゅうどう, 柔道
art of weaponless fencing

KARATE: からて, 空手
art of weaponless self-defense

GORUFU: ゴルフ
golf

SAAFIN: サーフィン
surfing

YAKYUU: やきゅう, 野球
baseball

BASUKETTO: バスケット
basketball

SUKII: スキー
skiing

TENISU: テニス
tennis

VIII. Nature

aki	kumori
ame	natsu
asa	sora
fuyu	taiyoo
hare	tenki
haru	tsuki
hiru	umi
hoshi	yama
kasa	yoru
kisetsu	yuki
kumo	

HARU: はる, 春 spring

NATSU: なつ, 夏 summer

UMI: うみ, 海
ocean

AKI: あき, 秋 autumn

FUYU: ふゆ, 冬 winter

81

HARE: はれ, 晴れ
sunny

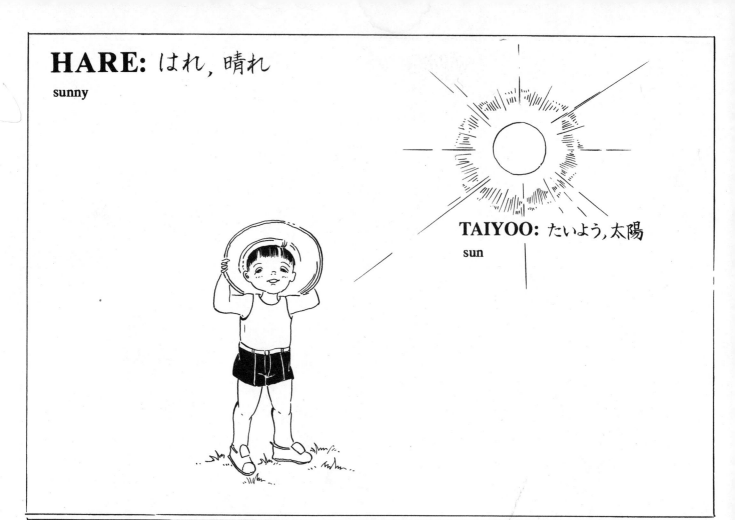

TAIYOO: たいよう, 太陽
sun

KUMORI: くもり, 曇り
cloudy

KUMO: くも, 曇
cloud

YAMA: やま, 山
mountain

AME: あめ, 雨

rain

KASA: かさ, 傘

umbrella

YUKI: ゆき, 雪

snow

HIRU: ひる, 昼
daytime

SORA: そら, 空
sky

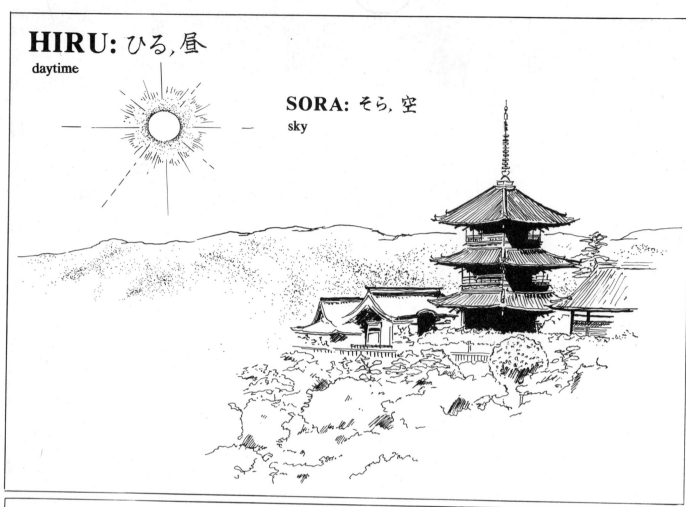

YORU: よる, 夜
night

HOSHI: ほし, 星
star

TSUKI: つき, 月
moon

IX. Body

ago	me
ashi	mimi
atama	mune
choo	noo
hana	onaka, hara
(o) heso	oshiri
hone	senaka
kami, ke	shinzoo
kao	te
kata	tsume
karada	ude
kanzoo	yubi

KARADA: からだ, 体
body

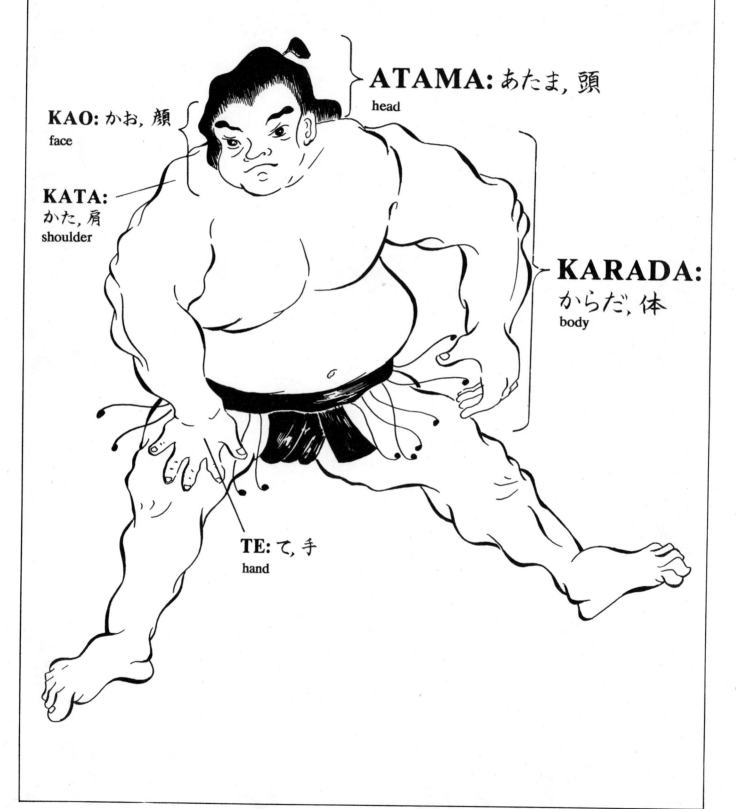

ATAMA: あたま, 頭
head

KAO: かお, 顔
face

KATA:
かた, 肩
shoulder

KARADA:
からだ, 体
body

TE: て, 手
hand

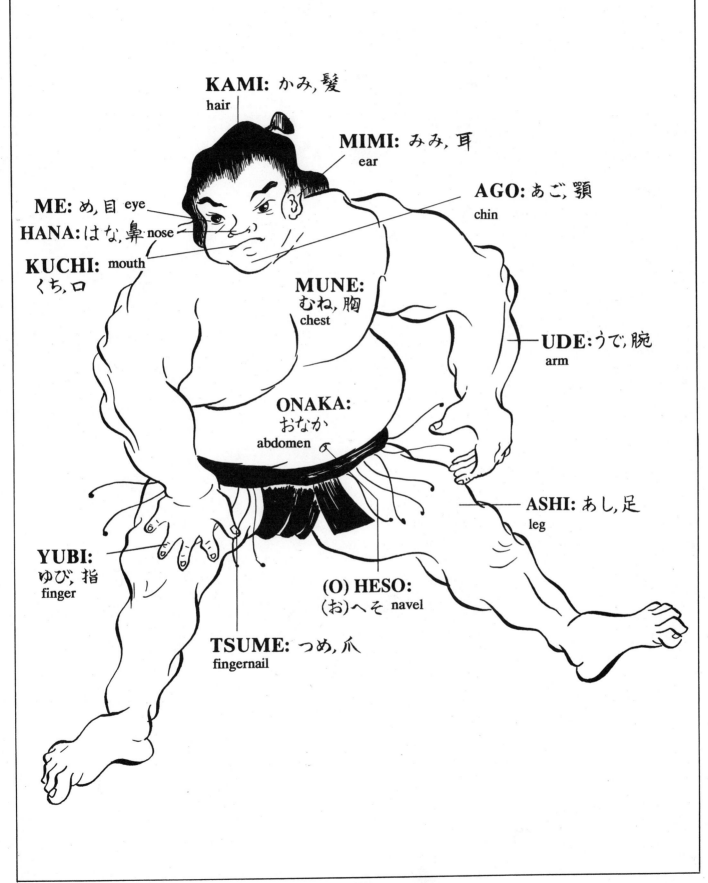

KAMI: かみ, 髪
hair

MIMI: みみ, 耳
ear

AGO: あご, 顎
chin

ME: め, 目 eye
HANA: はな, 鼻 nose
KUCHI: mouth
くち, 口

MUNE:
むね, 胸
chest

UDE: うで, 腕
arm

ONAKA:
おなか
abdomen

ASHI: あし, 足
leg

YUBI:
ゆび, 指
finger

(O) HESO:
(お)へそ navel

TSUME: つめ, 爪
fingernail

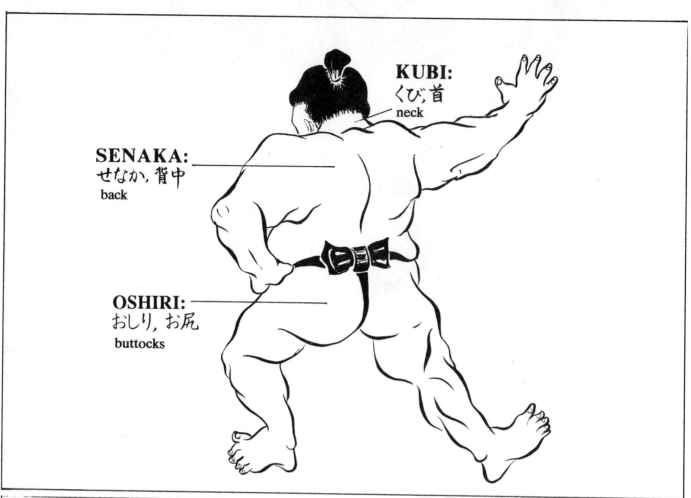

KUBI: くび, 首
neck

SENAKA:
せなか, 背中
back

OSHIRI:
おしり, お尻
buttocks

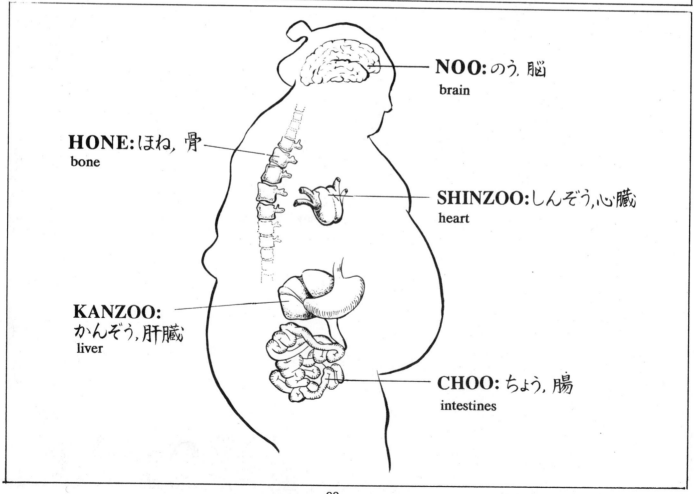

NOO: のう, 脳
brain

HONE: ほね, 骨
bone

SHINZOO: しんぞう, 心臓
heart

KANZOO:
かんぞう, 肝臓
liver

CHOO: ちょう, 腸
intestines

X. Numbers

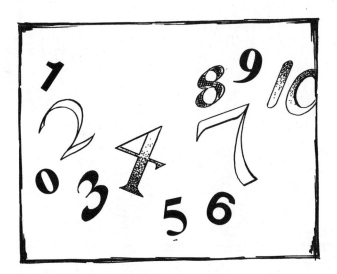

ichi	juu
ni	juu-ichi
san	juu-ni
shi, yon	ni-juu
go	san-juu
roku	hyaku
shichi, nana	sen
hachi	rei, zero
ku, kyuu	

ICHI 1: いち、一
one

NI 2: に、二
two

SAN 3: さん, 三
three

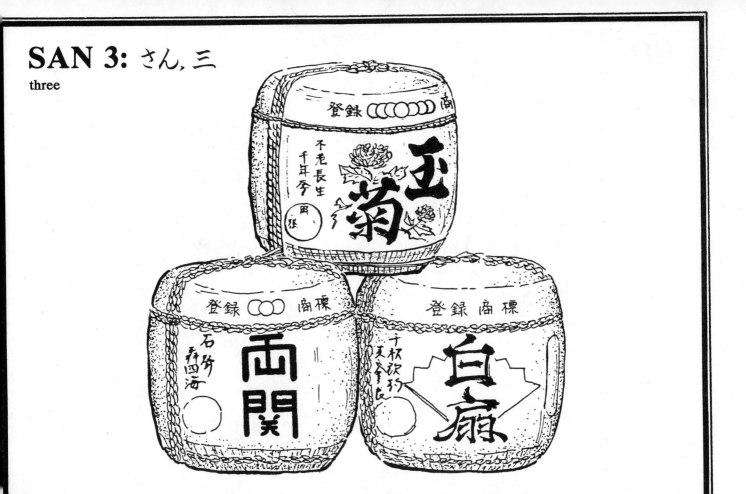

SHI 4: し, 四
four

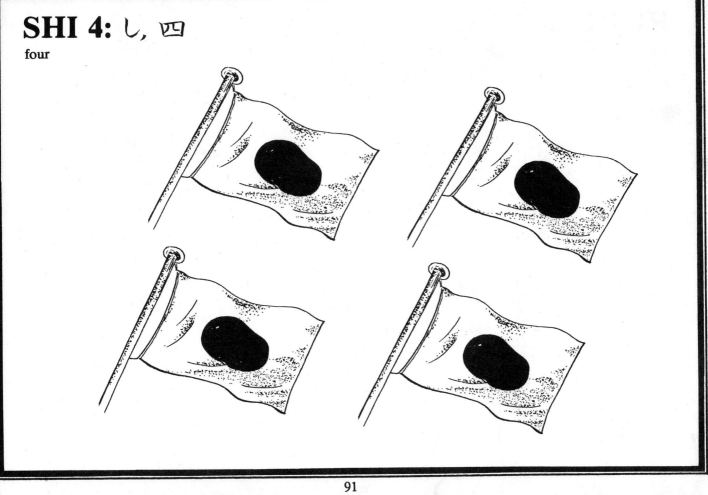

GO 5: ご, 五

five

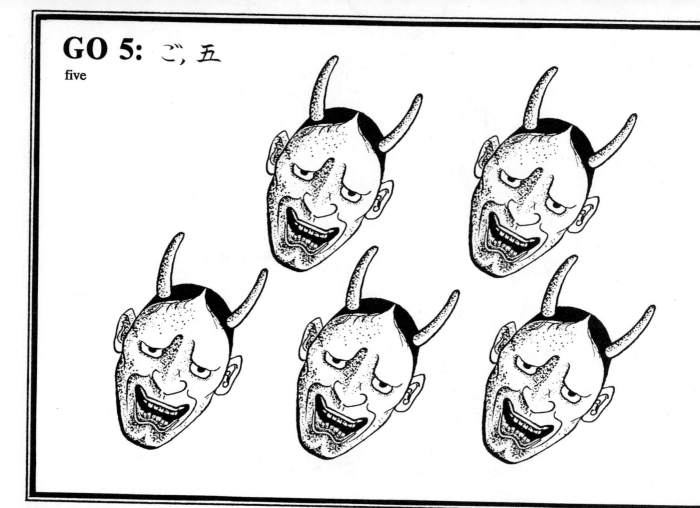

ROKU 6: ろく, 六

six

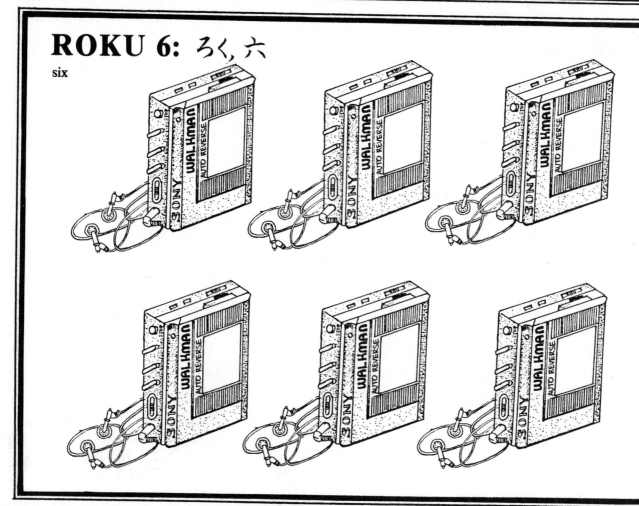

SHICHI 7:
しち, 七
seven

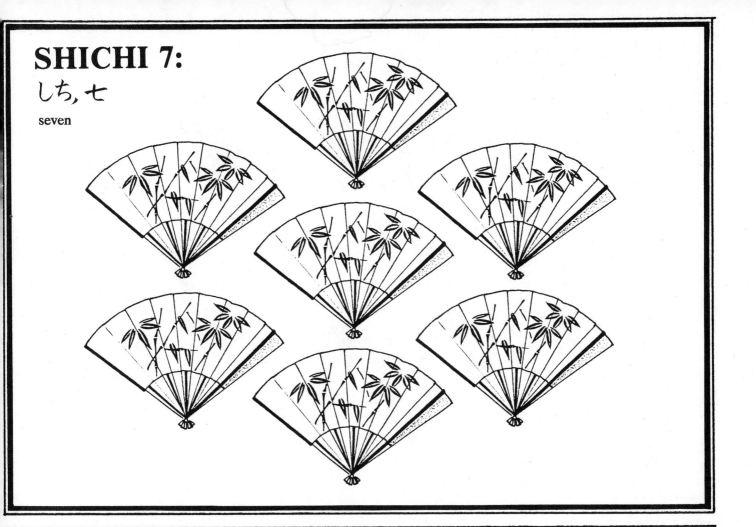

HACHI 8: はち, 八
eight

KU 9: く, 九
nine

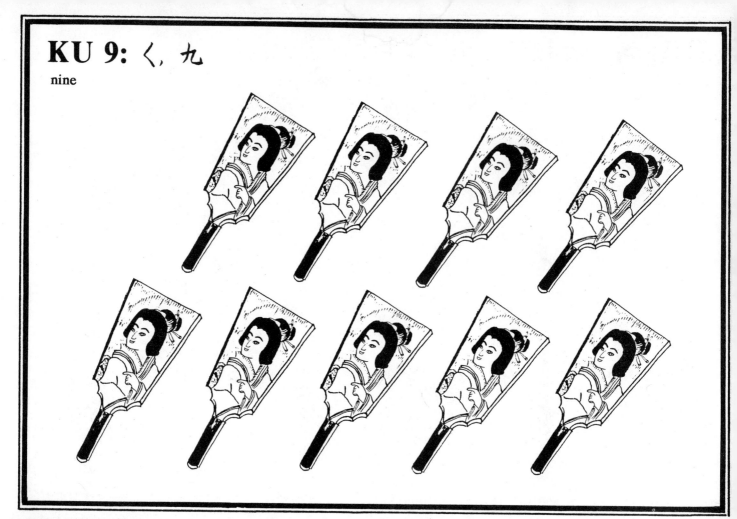

JUU 10:じゅう, 十
ten

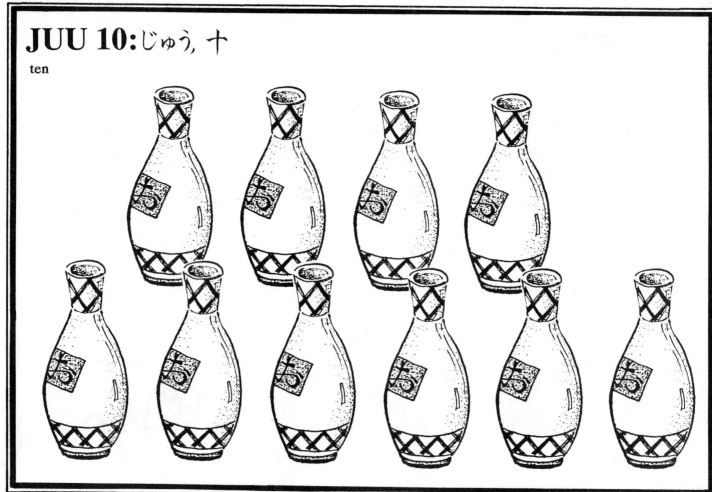

94

JUU-ICHI 11: じゅういち, 十一

eleven

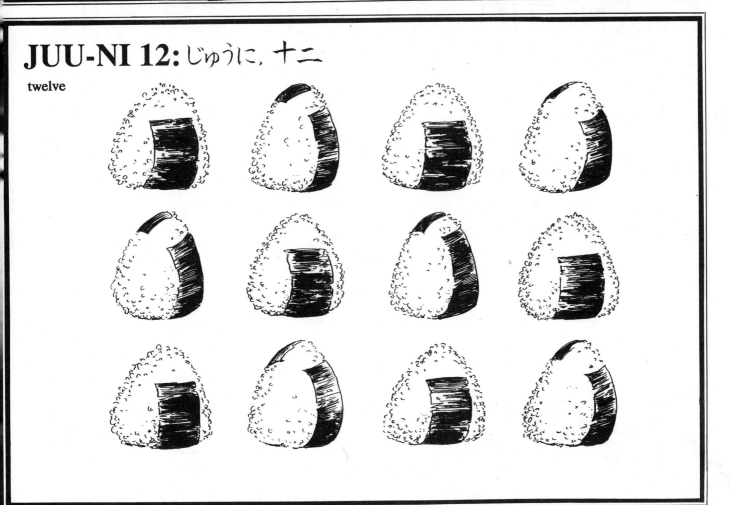

JUU-NI 12: じゅうに, 十二

twelve

ZERO: ゼロ
zero

0

NI-JUU: にじゅう, 二十
twenty

20

SAN-JUU: さんじゅう, 三十
thirty

30

HYAKU: ひゃく, 百
hundred

100

SEN: せん, 千
thousand

1000

XI. Greetings and
Daily Expressions

Arigatoo (gozaimasu).
Doo itashimashite.
Gomennasai.
Hajimemashite.
Itte kimasu.
Itte rasshai.
Jaa mata (ne).
Konbanwa.
Konnichiwa.
Ohayoo (gozaimasu).
Okaerinasai.
(O)namae wa.
Oyasuminasai.
Sayoonara.
Tadaima.

98

XI. GREETINGS & DAILY EXPRESSIONS

1. **Ohayoo (gozaimasu).** Good morning.
2. **Konnichiwa.** Hello.
3. **Konbanwa.** Good evening.
4. **Oyasuminasai.** Good night.
5. **Doozo** Here you are.
6. **Arigatoo (gozaimasu).** Thank you (very much).
7. **Doo itashimashite.** You are welcome.
8. **Gomennasai.** I am sorry. Excuse me.
9. **Hajimemashite.** How do you do?
10. **(O)namae wa.** What is your name?
11. **Itte kimasu.** I am leaving. (Said by a person as leaving home.)
12. **Itte rasshai.** So long. (This is the reply to **Itte kimasu.**)
13. **Tadaima.** I am back. (Said by a person on returning home.)
14. **Okaerinasai.** Welcome home. (This is the reply to **Tadaima.**)
15. **Sayoonara.** Goodbye.
16. **Jaa mata(ne).** See you then.
17. **Mata ashita.** See you tomorrow.
18. **Itadakimasu.** I will receive the meal.(Used before eating or drinking.)
19. **Gochisoosama (deshita).** Thank you for the meal. (Used after eating or drinking.)
20. **Chotto mattekudasai.** Wait just a moment, please.
21. **Moo ichido (onegaishimasu).** Once more (please).

Japanese Glossary

ageru — to give
ago — chin, jaw
aka — red
akachan — baby
akeru — to open
aki — autumn
ame — rain
anata — you
ane — (my) older sister
ani — (my) older brother
ao — blue
aruku — to walk
asa — morning
ashi — foot, leg
atama — head
atarashii — new
atsui — 1.hot 2.thick

bangoo — number
basu — bus
basutei — bus stop
basuketto — basketball
benkyo (o) suru — to study
(o)bentoo — box lunch
boku — I (used by boys)
bonsai — miniature potted plant
booshi — hat
burausu — blouse
byooin — hospital

chawan — rice bowl
chichi — (my) father
chiisai — small
chikaku — near
chikatetsu —subway
choo — intestines
chuugakusei — junior high
              school student
daidokoro — kitchen
daigakusei — college student
denki — electricity, electric light
densha — electric train
dentoo — tradition
denwa — telephone
denwa (o) suru — to call up
dooro — road, street

e — picture
eki — train station
enpitsu — pencil

fuku — clothes
fune — ship
furui — old
futon — comforter
fuyu — winter

gaijin, gaikokujin — foreigner

gakkoo — school
genkan — entrance hall
geta — wooden clogs
ginkoo — bank
go — five (5)
gohan — cooked rice, meal
gorufu — golf
goryooshin — (your) parents
goshujin — (your) husband

ha(ppa) — leaf
hachi — eight (8)
haha — (my) mother
haku — to put on
hana — 1.flower 2.nose
hanasu — to speak, to talk
hankachi — handkerchief
haru — spring
hashi — chopstick(s)
hashiru — to run
hataraku — to work
hayai — fast
(o)heso — navel
hidari — left
hikooki — plane
hikui — low, short
hiraku — to open
hiru — daytime
hon — book
hoshi — star
hyaku — hundred (100)

ichi — one (1)
ie — house
ii — good
ike — pond
iku — to go
imooto — (my) younger sister
imootosan — (your) younger sister
ishi — stone, rock
isu — chair

jidoosha — automobile
jisho — dictionary
jitensha — bicycle
juu — ten (10)
juu—ichi — eleven (11)
juu—ni — twelve (12)
juudoo — art of weaponless
          fencing

kaban — bag
kaeru — to return
kaku — to write
kami — 1.paper 2.hair
kanai — (my) wife
kangaeru — to think, to conceive
kanzoo — liver

kao — face
karada — body
karate — art of weaponless
          self—defence
karui — light
kasa — umbrella
kata — shoulder
kau — to buy
kazoku — family
keisatsu — police station
kendoo — Japanese art of
          self—defence
ki — tree
kiiro — yellow
kiku — to listen, to hear
kimono — Japanese robe,
          Japanese clothing
kippu — ticket
kirei(na) — beautiful, clean
kiru — to wear
kisetsu — season
kisha — freight train
kitanai — dirty
kitte — stamp
kodomo — child
kookoosei — senior high
            school student
kokuban — blackboard
kooen — park
koosaten — intersection
koppu — glass
ku, kyu — nine (9)
kubi — neck
kuchi — mouth
kudamono — fruit
kumo — cloud
kumori — cloudy
kuru — to come
kuruma — car
kushi — comb
kusuri — medicine
kutsu — shoes
kutsushita — socks
kuukoo — airport
kyoodai — brothers and sisters

machi — town, city
mado — window
mae — front
makura — pillow
me — eye
megane — eyeglasses
midori — green
migi — right
mijikai — short
mimi — ear
miru — to see, to look
miso shiru — soybean paste soup

morau – to receive
Moshi moshi. -- Hello.
  (in a telephone conversation)
mune – chest
murasaki – purple
musuko(san) – son
musume(san) – daughter
muzukashii – difficult

nagai – long
naka – inside
natsu – summer
neru – to sleep, to go to sleep
ni – two (2)
ni-juu – twenty (20)
nihonjin – Japanese people
niku – meat
ningyoo – doll
ninja – Japanese assassin
niwa – garden
nomimono – beverage, drink
nomu – to drink
norimono – transportation
noru – to get on
noo – brain
nugu – to take off

oba(san) – aunt
obaasan – (your) grandmother
obi – belt, sash
ocha – tea
ofuro – bath
oishii – tasty, delicious
oji(san) – uncle
ojiisan – (your) grandfather
okaasan – (your) mother
okane – money
okiru – to get up
okusan – (your) wife
omoi – heavy
omoshiroi – interesting, funny
onaka – stomach, belly, abdomen
oneesan – (your) older sister
oniisan – (your) older brother
onna – female
onna no hito – woman
onna no ko – girl
ookii – big, large
origami – paper-folding
oriru – to get off
oshieru – to teach
oshiri – buttocks
osoi – slow
ootobai – motorcycle
otearai – bathroom, toilet
otoko – male
otoko no hito – man
otoko no ko – boy
otona – adult

otoosan – (your) father
otooto – (my) younger brother
otooto(san) – (your) younger brother
owan – soup cup

rei – zero (0)
roku – six (6)
roojin – old person
ryooshin – (my) parents

saafin – surfing
sakana – fish
(o)sake – Japanese rice wine
samui – cold, chilly
samurai – Japanese swordsman,
      member of the warrior class
san – three (3)
san-juu – thirty (30)
sara – dish
(o)sashimi – raw fish
seito – student, pupil
sen – thousand (1000)
senaka – back (part of the body)
sensei – teacher
shatsu – shirt
shi – four (4)
shichi – seven (7)
shiken – test, examination
shimeru – to shut
shinbun – newspaper
shingoo – traffic light
shinkansen – bullet train
shinzoo – heart
shiro – white
shita – below, under
shizuka(na) – quiet
shodoo, shuuji – calligraphy
shoogakusei – elementary school
      student
shoogun – general
shujin – (my) husband
sora – sky
soto – outside
sukaato – skirt
sukii – skiing
sukiyaki – beef cooked
      with vegetables
sumoo – Japanese wrestling
(o)sushi – vinegared rice
      with raw fish
suupaa – supermarket
suwaru – to sit

tabemono – food
taberu – to eat
taiyoo – sun
takai – 1.high, tall
      2.expensive
tamago – egg

tatsu – to stand up
te – hand
tegami – letter
tenisu – tennis
tenki – weather
tenpura – deep-fried fish
      and vegetables
terebi – television, TV
tokei – watch, clock
tomodachi – friend
tooku – far
(o)toshiyori – old person
toshokan – library
tsukemono – pickled vegetables
tsuki – moon
tsukue – desk
tsumaranai – boring
tsume – fingernail
tsumetai – cold (to the touch)
tsuyoi – strong

ude – arm
ue – above, top, on
umi – sea, ocean
uru – to sell
urusai – noisy
ushiro – back, rear
usui – thin
utau – to sing

warau – to laugh
warui – bad
watashi – I
watashitachi – we

yakitori – grilled chicken
      on a stick
yakkyoku – pharmacy
yakyuu – baseball
yama – mountain
yane – roof
yasai – vegetable
yasashii – easy
yoofuku – clothes
yomu – to read
yoru – night
yowai – weak
yubi – finger
yuubinkyoku – post office
yukata – summer cotton
      kimono
yuki – snow
yunomi – tea cup

zero – zero (0)
zoori – sandals
zubon – pants, trousers

English Glossary

abdomen – onaka, hara
above – ue
adult – otona
airport – kuukoo
arm – ude
aunt – oba(san)
automobile – jidoosha
autumn – aki

baby – akachan
back – 1.ushiro 2.senaka
bad – warui
bag – kaban
bank – yuubinkyoku
baseball – yakyuu
basketball – basuketto
bath – ofuro
bathroom – otearai, toire
beautiful – kirei(na)
below – shita
beverage – nomimono
bicycle – jitensha
big – ookii
blackboard – kokuban
blue – ao
body – karada
book – hon
boring – tsumaranai
boy – otoko no ko
brain – noo
bullet train – shinkansen
bus – basu
bus stop – basutei
buttocks – oshiri

car – kuruma
chair – isu
cheap – yasui
chest – mune
child – kodomo
chin – ago
chopstick(s) – hashi
city – machi
clean – kirei(na)
clock – tokei
clothes – fuku, yoofuku
cloud – kumo
cloudy – kumori
cold – samui (feeling)
　　　　 tsumetai (touching)
college student – daigakusei
comb – kushi
comforter – futon

daughter – musume(san)
daytime – hiru
delicious – oishii
desk – tsukue

dictionary – jisho, jiten
difficult – muzukashii
dirty – kitanai
dish – sara
doll – ningyoo
door – to
drink – nomimono
ear – mimi
easy – yasashii
egg – tamago
eight (8) – hachi
electricity, – denki
　electric light
electric train – densha
elementary school – shoogakusei
　student
eleven (11) – juu–ichi
entrance hall – genkan
examination – shiken
expensive – takai
eye – me
eyeglasses – megane

face – kao
family – kazoku
far – tooku
fast – hayai
father – chichi, otoosan
female – onna
finger – ubi
fingernail – tsume
fish – sakana
five (5) – go
flower – hana
food – tabemono
foot – ashi
foreigner – gaijin, gaikokujin
four (4) – shi, yon
freight train – kisha
front – mae
fruit – kudamono

garden – niwa
girl – onna no ko
glass – koppu
golf – gorufu
good – ii
grandfather – sofu, ojiisan
grandmother – sobo, obaasan
green – midori

hair – kami, ke
hand – te
hat – booshi
head – atama
heart – shinzoo
heavy – omoi
Hello. – Moshi moshi.

high – takai
high school student – kookoosei
hospital – byooin
hot – atsui
hundred (100) – hyaku
husband – shujin, goshujin

I – watashi
inside – naka
interesting – omoshiroi
intersection – koosaten
intestines – choo

Japanese person – nihonjin
junior high school – chuugakusei
　student

kindergartener – yoochienji
kitchen – daidokoro

large – ookii
leaf – ha(ppa)
leg – ashi
letter – tegami
library – toshokan
light – karui
liver – kanzoo
long – nagai

male – otoko
man – otoko no hito
meat – niku
medicine – kusuri
money – okane
moon – tsuki
morning – asa
mother – haha, okaasan
motorcycle – ootobai
mouth – kuchi

navel – (o)heso
near – chikaku
neck – kubi
new – atarashii
newspaper – shinbun
night – yoru
nine (9) – ku, kyuu
noisy – yakamashii
nose – hana
number – kazu, bangoo

ocean – umi
old – furui
old person – roojin, (o)toshiyori
older brother – ani, oniisan
older sister – ane, oneesan
one (1) – ichi
outside – soto

pants – zubon, pantsu
paper – kami
parent(s) – oya, goryooshin
park – kooen
pencil – enpitsu
pharmacy – yakkyoku
picture – e
pillow – makura
plane – hikooki
police station – keisatsu
pond – ike
post office – yuubinkyoku
purple – murasaki

quiet – shizuka(na)

rain – ame
raw fish – (o)sashimi
red – aka
right – migi
road – dooro
rock – ishi
roof – yane

sandal – zoori
school – gakkoo
sea – umi
season – kisetsu
seven (7) – shichi, nana
ship – fune
shirt – shatsu
shoe(s) – kutsu
short – mijikai
shoulder – kata
six (6) – roku
ski, skiing – sukii
skirt – sukaato
sky – sora
slow – osoi
small – chiisai
snow – yuki
sock(s) – kutsushita
son – musuko(san)
spring – haru
stamp – kitte
star – hoshi
street – michi, dooro
strong – tsuyoi
student – seito, gakusei
subway – chikatetsu
summer – natsu
sun – taiyoo
sunny – hare
supermarket – suupaa
surfing – saafin

tall – takai
tasty – oishii
tea – ocha
teacher – sensei
telephone – denwa
ten (10) – juu
tennis – tenisu
test – shiken
thick – atsui
thin – usui
thirty (30) – san–juu
thousand (1000) – sen
three (3) – san
ticket – kippu
to buy – kau
to call up – denwa suru
to come – kuru
to drink – nomu
to eat – taberu
to get off – oriru
to get on – noru
to get up – okiru
to give – ageru
to go –iku
to hear – kiku
to laugh – warau
to listen – kiku
to look – miru
to open – akeru
to put on – 1.kiru 2.haku
to receive – morau
to return – kaeru
to run – hashiru
to see – miru
to sell – uru
to sing – utau
to sit down – suwaru
to sleep – neru
to stand up – tatsu
to study – benkyoo (o) suru
to take off – nugu
to talk – hanasu
to teach – oshieru
to think – kangaeru
to walk – aruku
to wear – kiru
to work – hataraku,
          shigoto (o) suru
to write – kaku
town – machi
tradition – dentoo
traffic light – shingoo
train station – eki
tree – ki
twelve (12) – juu–ni
twenty (20) – ni–juu
two (2) – ni

umbrella – kasa
uncle – oji(san)

vegetable – yasai

watch – tokei
water – mizu
we –watashitachi
weak – yowai
weather – tenki
white – shiro
wife – kanai, okusan
window – mado
winter – fuyu
woman – onna no hito

yellow – kiiro
you – anata
younger brother – otooto,
                  otootosan
younger sister – imooto,
                 imootosa

zero (0) – rei, zero